Good Night Little Doctor

BY DR. INTERGALACTIC

PICTURES BY UGURKOSE

AD ASTRA MEDIA, LLC • VIRGINIA

www.adastrasteammedia.com

ISBN: 978-1-0878-7894-2
IMPRINT: INDEPENDENTLY PUBLISHED

Copyright © 2021 Ad Astra Media, LLC. All rights reserved. Independently published in the United States by Ad Astra Media, LLC and Jose Morey.

Good night little doctor

Sleep tight little doctor

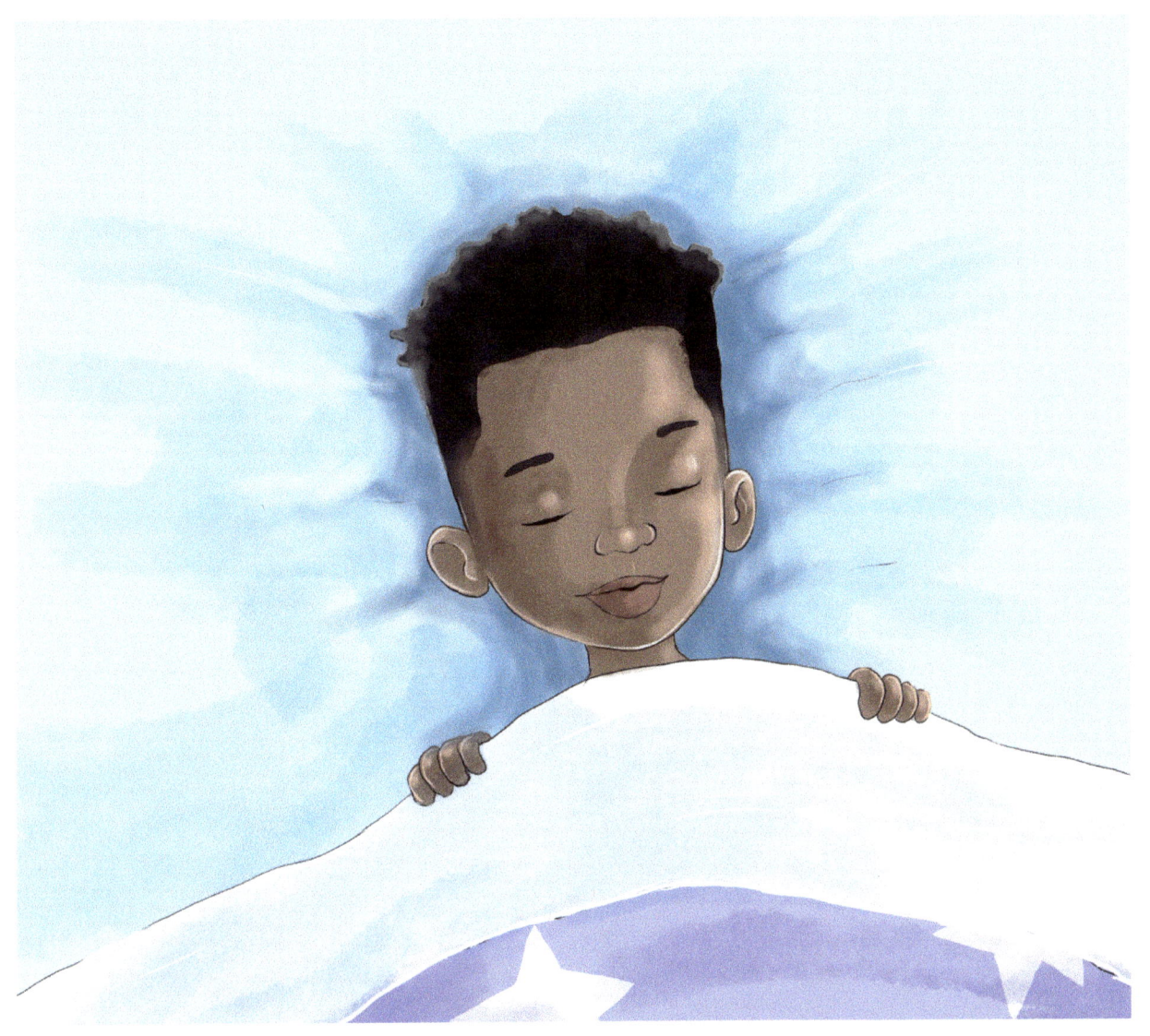

You need to get your rest

For tomorrow you need to be your best

Many patients there are to see

How many?

Maybe one or two or three?

Bones to fix and medicines to give

You are important, little doctor

for the people to live

Good night little doctor
Sleep tight little doctor

Sleep is important to rest your hands
Who cures the sick? Well of course, you can!

Doctors fix cancer and make vaccines

They make sure that ears and noses stay clean

They treat kids and grandparents, moms and dads

They make you feel better when you feel bad

Good night little doctor

Sleep tight little doctor

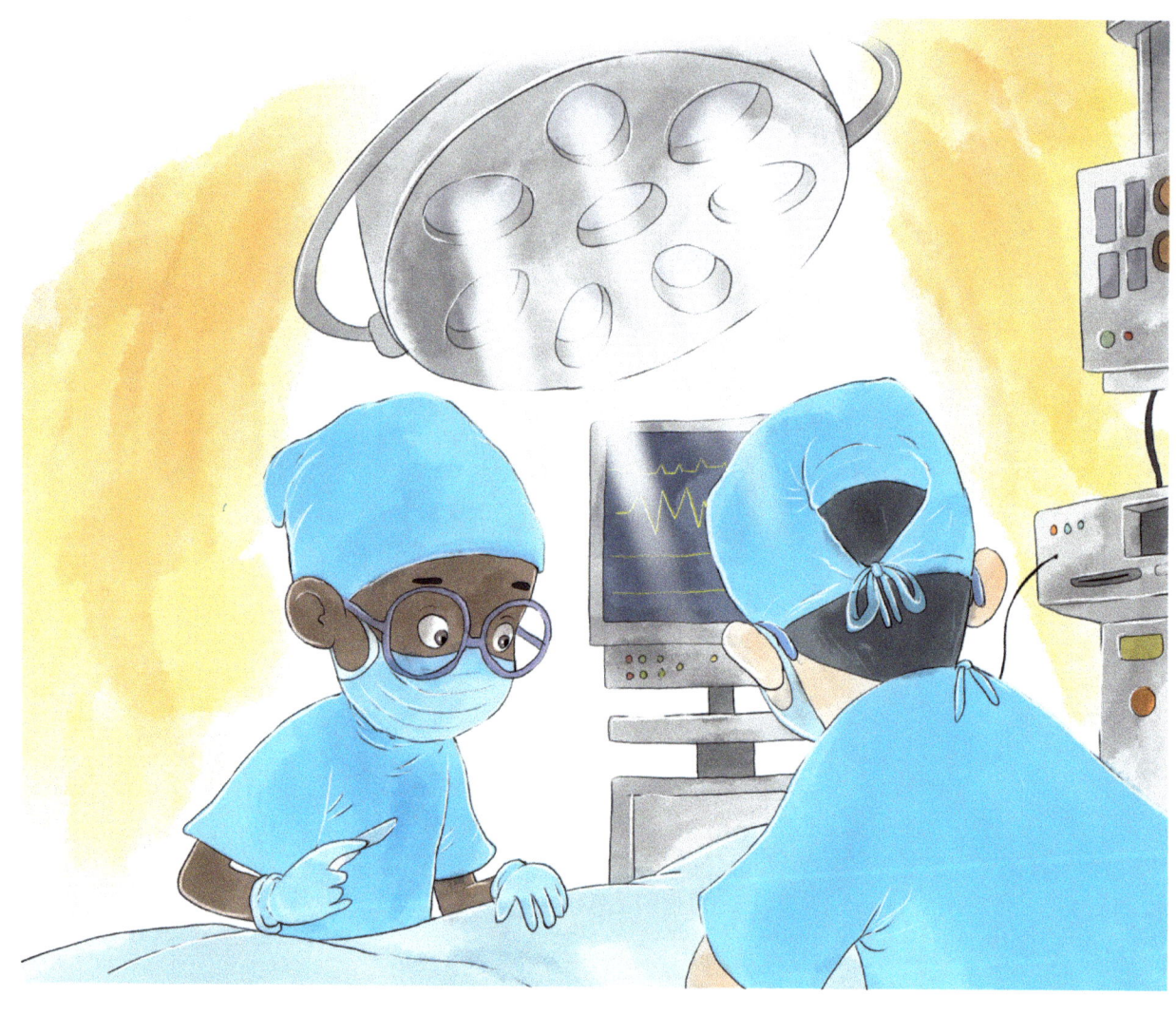

Tomorrow you might be in surgery...

Where you will cure other little ones,

like you and like me

You might need a great big bandage too...

For doctors fix all kinds of boo-boos!

Or maybe you will give a shot

Shots may hurt a little...
but they sure help a lot!

Good night little doctor

Sleep tight little doctor

Doctors come in all sizes and shapes

They say to be kind and eat all your grapes

There are small doctors, big doctors
Boy doctors and girl doctors

Doctors can speak English and Spanish, Igbo and French – this helps them speak with all the patients on their rosters

Doctors come from cities and islands,
far and wide
Doctors can skateboard, sing,
and surf the tides

Good night little doctor
Sleep tight little doctor

For tomorrow is another great day....

Ad Astra Media, LLC is a Latino owned S.T.E.A.M. media and edutainment company seeking to renew a faith in facts and reason and uplift underserved and minority communities by providing them with scientific role models in science, technology, engineering, art and math (S.T.E.A.M.) to which they can aspire. We are composed of individuals with experience at all levels of T.V. and commercial media production, running from traditional television services on Spanish and English networks all the way to leading streaming services and film studios. We have memorandums of understanding with digital animation studios supported by the Space Foundation and who have worked with Disney and Pixar.

 See what is up next on our diverse multilingual S.T.E.A.M. children's series by Dr. Intergalactic,

Good Night Little Astronomer  What Are Tears For, Momma?

www.ingramcontent.com/pod-product-compliance
Lightning Source LLC
Chambersburg PA
CBHW061156010526
44118CB00027B/2989